iLLUMINATIONS

REFLECTING OUR PAST
LIGHTING OUR FUTURE

Celebrating
125
years
First
Presbyterian
Church
1885•2010

FIRST PRESBYTERIAN CHURCH
TULSA † OKLAHOMA

First Presbyterian Church was organized on October 5, 1885. Annie Coe Kerr — wife of our first pastor, Charles W. Kerr — determined the architectural style of the present buildings, English Gothic, and monitored the construction.

THE ARCHITECT WAS J.S. PARR OF OKLAHOMA CITY. J.M. BERRY WAS CHAIR OF THE TRUSTEES AT THE DEDICATION IN 1925.

© 2010 by First Presbyterian Church of Tulsa

All rights reserved. First Edition. First printing

New Revised Standard Version Bible, copyright 1989, Division of Christian Education of the National Council of the Churches of Christ in the United States of America. Used by permission. All rights reserved.

Project coordinator: Joan Williams Hoar
Photo editor: Tom Gilbert
Editor: Mark Brown
Book and cover design: Carl Brune

Printed by die Keure, Bruges, Belgium

ISBN 978-0-615-37065-1

First Presbyterian Church, Tulsa, Oklahoma
709 S. Boston Ave, Tulsa OK 74119

firstchurchtulsa.org

PAGE I
PRAISE THE LORD ROSE WINDOW

Gift of Mr. and Mrs. David (Cassie) Temple.
Installed 1981

PSALM 148:1

ENTRY VESTIBULE

FRONTISPIECE
The Lord's Prayer : Our Father who art in heaven . . .

MATTHEW 6:9–13, LUKE 11:2–4

SANCTUARY : SW UPPER BALCONY DOORS

TITLE PAGE
The Lord's Prayer : For thine is the kingdom, the power, and the glory . . .

MATTHEW 6:9–13, LUKE 11:2–4

SANCTUARY : NW UPPER BALCONY DOORS

CONTENTS

Honor and majesty surround him;
Strength and beauty are in his sanctuary.

PSALM 96:6

WISEMAN ROSE WINDOW
Designed by Willet Stained Glass
Studio Inc.

Donated by Bill Wiseman Jr. in
honor of his father, Dr. William
Wiseman, Pastor Emeritus.

Installed 1996

SANCTUARY : WEST WALL

FOREWORD

This pictorial account reveals our church and two additional buildings as they stand today . . . places of worship, study, fellowship, missions, celebration and remembrance. Here, where the city was born and our heritage began, First Presbyterian Church of Tulsa stands as a lasting tribute to God, to great men and women, and to an eternally profound faith of vision and ideals.

First Church has indeed evolved from its humble beginnings as a one-room school house at Fourth Street and Boston Avenue. In 1911, it moved into a newly constructed brick building of Greek Revival style. Since 1925, our home has been at 7th Street and Boston Avenue. It has grown into a campus that includes:

THE SANCTUARY : A 16th-century cathedral-style building with English Gothic design influences.

THE BERNSEN COMMUNITY LIFE CENTER : A historic, Art Deco Masonic Temple building — 700 South Boston Avenue — acquired in 1994 for all ages to enjoy sports, entertainment and worship.

THE POWERHOUSE : A 1929 Prairie Eclectic-style building — 223 East 8th Street — updated to a contemporary atmosphere for our youth.

Transformation, it seems, is the lifeblood of this church — it has been achieved with the financial and strategic foresight of those who have gone before us and is the impetus that guides us forward as we continue to meet the needs of a dedicated congregation.

First Church is blessed with a beauty of a rare order. Each Sunday, its sanctuary echoes with marvelous music, spoken word, and bountiful Biblical symbolism. Every day, our carillon of 32 bronze bells rings angelic high notes and bold low ones, hammering out the Westminster chimes and seasonal hymns that can be heard up and down the avenues. Every day, church members and citizens gather, study and engage amid an array of art and adornment. The magnificence recalls the tradition of an inspired religious age. Our walls transcend time and place and, within them, a member of this church is part of an ageless community of faith, constantly renewed, and ever growing in strength and hope in God.

Woven throughout this book are photographs of stained glass, sculpture, textiles, paintings, and carvings, each a story within the larger narrative. We are surrounded by God's love for us within our interior and exterior walls of worship. Our heritage is richly steeped in His infinite blessings.

As we reach beyond the threshold, we give thanks for the forethought of a devoted congregation. Each person has shared the dream of First Church's future as it embarks on new construction — and another transformation. Just as we reflect on our past, we will light the future of generations to follow within the splendor of our refreshed walls and new spaces.

Remember the church in your prayers. Join with me as we thank God for the privilege of serving Him in such a place. Be illumined as you enjoy new discoveries and kindle remembrances. Visit them within these pages; and in person, with a deep sense of gratitude and exuberance.

In Christ's name,
ELAINE G. HORKEY, *Elder*
Chair, 125th Anniversary Celebration

THE GOOD SAMARITAN
Ann Willet Stained Glass Atelier, Spring House, Pennsylvania. 1984

The Windows given to the Glory of God in memory of Beloved Family Members by Annelle Chandler McAdams, 1985

LUKE 10:29–34

ELEVATOR LOBBY

ACKNOWLEDGEMENTS

I have always known I would write a book. I just did not know it would be a book of liturgical art. My deep appreciation and love of religious art began as a child when I turned the pages in our family Bible. Beautiful images from the Middle Ages, Renaissance and Baroque periods were etched in my memory. In 2006, Reverend Richard K. Davis asked me to document the church art. I am grateful for the opportunity to employ my love of inspiring art in this publication, *Illuminations*, in celebration of the 125th anniversary of Tulsa's First Presbyterian Church.

No task of this size could be completed without many generous contributors. Thanks especially to Nancy C. Chandler, who worked tirelessly with me over a two-year period. Ellen Vester joined us toward the end and added greatly to the research.

Many thanks go to Amy Pulliam, the librarian at Willet Hauser Architectural Glass, who researched and answered many questions about the Willet windows.

David Crowell, our archivist, was never too busy to check a fact or confirm a detail. The Reverends Warren Muller and Elaine Johnson and Director of Music Ministries Ron Pearson reviewed the copy and added insight. Director of Communications Meghan Beam devoted hours to promotion and technical assistance. Ken Busby, Executive Director Arts and Humanities Council, put me in touch with a valuable source of information. Gifted photographers Cindy Johnson, Tom Gilbert, Bruce Lytle, Jenette and Paul McEntire and Michelle Pollard are the reasons this publication succeeded. They gave generously of their time and expertise. Council Oaks principals Paulette Millichap and Sally Dennison steered us in the right direction early on. Sandy Curtis was invaluable when researching Bernsen Center items. A special thanks goes to my husband, Larry, for his patience.

Through their expertise and professionalism, Mark Brown, our editor, and Tom Gilbert, photography editor, ensured a quality work of art. Carl Brune, a professional publisher and layout designer, guided us through the publication process and designed the layout of the book.

The project would not have been possible, though, without the confidence and trust of Pastor Dr. James D. Miller and Elaine Horkey, Director of Planned Giving Ministries and our 125th Anniversary Celebration Chair.

My deep appreciation extends to each of you and to the many who added to the information with a name, date, or bit of history. You know who you are.

Blessings and prayers that this book will increase your awareness of the beauty that surrounds us, the generosity of those who came before us, and a deepened sense of responsibility of our commitment to the future.

JOAN WILLIAMS HOAR, *Elder*

THE FOUR SEEDS
Ann Willet Stained Glass Atelier, Spring House, Pennsylvania. 1984

The windows given to the Glory of God in memory of Beloved Family Members by Annelle Chandler McAdams, 1985

MATTHEW 13:3–9
ELEVATOR LOBBY

I ask that God illumine the eyes of your heart so that you may become aware of the hope to which He is calling you . . .

For the past 125 years, the preacher at First Church has climbed into the pulpit and offered a "prayer of illumination" just before preaching the sermon. It's a simple prayer asking God to use the sermon to shine the good news of Jesus Christ into the human heart.

The prayer behind this book is similar: that somehow — through the beauty of First Church's architecture and artwork, in the symbols etched in wood and the stories arranged in glass — the saving grace of Jesus Christ will be illumined, shining brightly for all to see.

You may have grown up as a cradle-roll member of First Church; you might have run through its halls as a student and explored every nook and cranny; you may have worshipped for years in the sanctuary. No matter. I'm quite sure that there is gospel beauty to be discovered in these pages that not even the longest living member will have seen: hidden treasures, right here among us, pointing to the grace of God in Jesus Christ.

May this book of gospel images and sacred beauty (all found on the FPC campus!) bless you in precisely that way. *Soli Deo Gloria!*

JAMES D. MILLER PhD
Pastor

PRAISE THE LORD ROSE
WINDOW

PSALM 148:12

VESTIBULE

HOW TO LOOK AT LITURGICAL ART

Artists employ symbols to instill their works with meaning. A knowledge of symbols is critical to understanding the visual arts.

In the era prior to widespread literacy, symbols in religious art were used to instruct, inspire and reinforce the faith among the followers.

The beautiful stained glass windows in European cathedrals served two purposes: they depicted the stories that sustained the faith; more immediately, they let in light – the "Light of God," the illumination.

The Kerr Chapel windows are examples of how symbols tell stories familiar in Christianity.

In the nativity window, the viewer sees the image of three individuals, each wearing specific colored dress. Notice also the lantern and the animals. In this scene, each color, plant, animal and object symbolizes something about the persons and event.

Although we refer to this as the nativity window, another very important symbol is part of the story. What is the Christ child lying on? Sheaves of wheat. From wheat comes flour, which makes bread. In this we see a symbol for communion, the Last Supper.

The companion window, immediately to the right — Christ with the children — includes a cluster of grapes in the lower left corner. Wine is the second element of the Eucharist.

To assist you in your "reading" of religious art, a list of symbols and their meanings is located on page 96.

As you study the many beautiful windows and other works of art at First Presbyterian Church, our prayer for you is that the meaning of our faith and heritage will be increased manyfold.

NATIVITY

Donated by Annelle Chandler McAdams
Installed September, 1979

LUKE 2:6–7

KERR CHAPEL

REJOICE

Rejoice, the Lord is King!
Your Lord and King adore;
Mortals, give thanks and sing,
And triumph evermore.
Lift up your heart,
Lift up your voice; rejoice;
Again I say, rejoice.

CHARLES WESLEY, 1746

I was glad when they said to me, "Let us go to the house of the Lord!"

PSALM 122:1

ROSE WINDOW

PSALM 148:14

VESTIBULE

Praise him with the sound of the trumpet;
praise him with the lyre and harp.

PSALM 150:3

THE CONTINUO ORGAN

This small portable is located at the rear of the sanctuary.

Gift of William H. Shambaugh in memory of his parents in 1993

THE KERR CHAPEL ORGAN

The original Kerr organ was given by the Mr. and Mrs. Class in 1954. The current Kerr Chapel organ was given by Mr. and Mrs. David (Sara Ann) Burton, in memory of her parents, Mr. and Mrs. Edward Sloan. Jan Keene refurbished the organ in memory of her mother, Marie Keene, 2007.

PREVIOUS PAGE.

LEFT : THE SANCTUARY ORGAN WAS BUILT BY AUSTIN ORGANS, INC. HARTFORD, CONN. Dedication was on January 12, 1969, with guest performer Frederick Swann, organist of The Riverside Church, New York City.

The organ includes 116 ranks (sets) of pipes, for a total of 6,642, ranging in length from nearly twenty feet to less than one inch. The main console has four manual keyboards and one pedal keyboard.

Gift of Mr. and Mrs. Robert C. Sharp.

TOP RIGHT : BELLS
A 32 bronze bell carillon crafted by the Fonderie Paccard of Annecy, France, represented in the USA by van Bergen Company, was dedicated on Sunday, December 2, 2007.

Major donors to the acquisition were Doris Maher and Pat Wheeler.

BELL TOWER

BOTTOM RIGHT : ORGAN CONSOLE

CHRIST, THE "LIGHT OF THE WORLD"

Jesus, the central figure of this focal window holds a lamp, but His countenance burns even more brightly. He is crowned the "Light of the World." The accompanying medallions each symbolize one of the I Ams, found in the Gospel of John. The words "I Am" at the top are enclosed first in a circle — the one God — then in a trefoil — the triune God. The new chancel window was part of the remodeling of the chancel area in the late 1960s, with dedication held on January 12, 1969.

DETAIL : CHRIST, THE LIGHT OF THE WORLD

Installed the week of December 4, 1967, following the renovation of 1965–67.

This window replaced the original window of the same design based on the famous painting by William Holman-Hunt, *The Light of the World.*

Donated by Mr. D.J. Tuepker in memory of his wife, Ardyth Tuepker.

CHANCEL

"I AM . . ."

THE ALPHA AND OMEGA
. . . the beginning and the ending of all.

THE MESSIAH
. . . accompanied by the scroll with the inscription I.N.R.I., Jesus of Nazareth,
King of the Jews, which was attached to the cross.
JOHN 4:25

THE LIVING WATER
. . . is that of Baptism, flowing like a river.
JOHN 4:13–14

THE BREAD OF LIFE
. . . is the wheat and a loaf.
JOHN 6:35, 51

THE TRUE VINE
. . . and grapes combine with the bread opposite
to form the elements of Communion.
JOHN 15:1

FROM ABOVE
. . . comes that light from heaven.
JOHN 6:51

THE CROSS OF FAITH
. . . is the way, the truth, and the life.
JOHN 14:6

THE ETERNAL ONE
. . . the sacred monogram – chi rho (XP) – for Jesus Christ
JOHN 17:24–25

THE RESURRECTION
. . . the mythical phoenix, which the ancients believed that, instead of dying,
set fire to her nest and rose rejuvenated from the flames.
JOHN 11:25–26

THE DOOR
. . . swings open in welcome.
Jesus is the door entered to be saved.
JOHN 10:7–11 (KJV)

THE SON OF GOD
. . . is shown by a triangle, again the Trinity.
JOHN 10:34–38 (KJV)

THE LORD AND MASTER
. . . is indicated by a royal crown.
JOHN 13:12–16

"for we preach not ourselves, but Christ Jesus the Lord; and ourselves your servants for Jesus' sake."
II Corinthians 4:5.

DETAIL : PULPIT INSCRIPTION

. . . for we preach not for ourselves, but Christ Jesus the Lord: and ourselves your servants for Jesus' sake.

II Corinthians 4:5

ABOVE : Celtic Cross at the foot of the pulpit

CHANCEL

PREVIOUS PAGE

LOWER LEFT :

Pulpit : The sanctuary pulpit is in the center of the chancel raised above all seating, as this is where the word of God is spoken. The three arches in relief are a repetitive motif inside each arch around the pulpit base. The eight-sided octagon shape represents the resurrection.

The original pulpit was a gift of Mr. and Mrs. Lawrence L. Dresser.

UPPER LEFT AND RIGHT:

Eagle Lectern
Given to the Glory of God and in loving memory of Sarah and Wilton O. Dixon by their son, James P. Dixon.

Eagle : Symbol of the resurrection of the Christian Spirit.
Rev. 4:6–8
Created by artists William R. Derrevere, Paul Moore and Dewayne Pass.

Chancel

PRESENT PAGE

LEFT : **Pulpit** : The pulpit in the Bernsen Community Life Center is a replica made for the 75th anniversary of an early pulpit by Rev. Ralph Lamb and carried across the Arkansas River from Red Fork. The original pulpit is on display in the Patterson Lounge. It holds the Lilah D. Lindsey Bible, named for a noted church teacher and civic leader.

RIGHT : **Pulpit and lectern** : The pulpit in the chapel is located to the south with the lectern on the north, an unusual arrangement in Presbyterian Churches.

Kerr Chapel

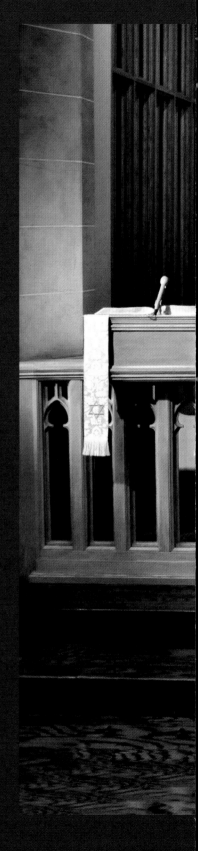

ABOVE : CHANCEL CLERGY SEATS : The needlepoint cushion on the left depicts the apostle Mark represented by the winged lion. On the right, the ship of salvation represents the Church. The ivy around the edge is evergreen and represents eternal life. The Roman numerals are 1885, the year First Church was founded.

The needlepoint cushions were crafted by a committee of members including Anne McCune, Amy Dodson, Diane Miller, Frances Patterson, Willie Hodges, Marcia Lansdown, Susan Diacon, Jean Lemmon, Jackie Allen, Pam Shaeffer and Ruth Huffman.

Your word is a lamp to my feet and a light to my path.

PSALM 119:105

DOOR LIGHTS

Door lights can be found in the entrances throughout the sanctuary. Symbols of parables are used nearest the pulpit, which is the source of teaching.

The two doors on the south at lower level show the house built on sand being washed away by the storm while the house on the rock stands unmoved. In one of the corresponding doors on the north are the talents. In the other, new wine is poured into old skins and consequently spills out. In the upper balcony six other parables are illustrated.

PARABLES

A HOUSE BUILT ON SAND

A HOUSE BUILT ON ROCKS

*The house built on sand crumbles as columns
are broken, while the house built on rock
survives the falling rain and churning waters.*

MATTHEW 7:27

SANCTUARY : MAIN FLOOR SE DOORS

PARABLES

THE TALENTS

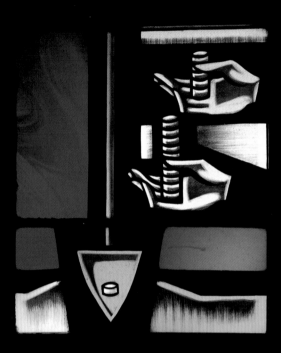

WISE AND FOOLISH VIRGINS

The coins are distributed to the servants with expectation of a greater return, but one servant uses a shovel and buries his single talent.

Matthew 25:29

SANCTUARY : MAIN FLOOR NE DOORS

The wise virgins maintain their lamps, but the foolish virgins allow their lamps to flicker out.

Matthew 25:18

SANCTUARY : BALCONY SE DOORS

PARABLES

THE THREE MEASURES

NEW WINE

Old wineskins are dry and cracked and will not contain the new wine.

MATTHEW 9:17

SANCTUARY : MAIN FLOOR NE DOORS

A small amount of yeast is sufficient for the three cups of flour.

MATTHEW 13:33

SANCTUARY : BALCONY SE DOORS

PARABLES

THE LOST AND FOUND SHEEP

SEPARATING THE NATIONS

The good shepherd uses his crook to save the lost sheep.

LUKE 15:4

SANCTUARY : BALCONY SE DOORS

Goats are separated from the sheep, with each sent to either heaven or hell.

MATTHEW 25:31–34

SANCTUARY : BALCONY SE DOORS

PARABLES

THE TREE

A tiny seed is the genesis of a great tree.

MATTHEW 13:31–32

SANCTUARY : BALCONY NE DOORS

THE KINGDOM CASTS A WIDE NET

Although many fish may be caught, only the good ones are kept.

MATTHEW 13:47–48

SANCTUARY : BALCONY NE DOORS

JESUS WORSHIPS IN THE TEMPLE ON THE SABBATH
Jesus teaches on the Sabbath.

LUKE 4:16–22

NARTHEX

JESUS TEACHES A LESSON OF FAITH
Jesus teaches a lesson of faith using lilies
and birds.

MATTHEW 6:26–29

NARTHEX

JESUS IS TAKEN TO THE TEMPLE BY HIS PARENTS.
Jesus at the age of twelve went with Mary and
Joseph to Jerusalem to the temple to celebrate the
Feast of the Passover.

LUKE 2:41

NARTHEX

JESUS IN THE TEMPLE WITH THE TEACHERS
Jesus is in the temple with the teachers, listening
to them and asking them questions. In this
representation, Jesus is listening to the elders,
asking questions rather than instructing.

LUKE 2:46

NARTHEX

THE ALPHA AND OMEGA
Ann Willet Stained Glass Atelier, Spring House,
Pennsylvania, 1983.

REVELATION 22:13

NARTHEX

JESUS AND NICODEMUS

JOHN 3:1

NARTHEX

JESUS IN THE HOME OF MARY AND MARTHA

JOHN 11:1; LUKE 10:38–42

NARTHEX

PRAYER

Prayer connects us to God. Through prayer we acknowledge God's power and goodness and our own neediness and dependence. Prayer may be a petition, thanksgiving, worship or confession. Prayer may be individual or communal, given in public or private.

The Lord's Prayer is perhaps the best-known prayer in Christianity. Two versions of it occur in the Gospels – in Matthew 6:9-13, as part of the discourse on ostentation, a section of the Sermon on the Mount; and in Luke 11:2-4.

As for you, O LORD, you will not restrain your mercy from me; your steadfast love and your faithfulness will ever preserve me!

PSALM 40:11

THE LATIN CROSS ON TABLE
Created, crafted and donated
by Dr. George Coe.

KERR CHAPEL
JOHN 19:17–18

THE LORD'S PRAYER

OUR FATHER WHO ART IN HEAVEN

HALLOWED BE THY NAME

The triune God is represented by a triangle. God's hand reaches from heaven toward earth in benediction.

SANCTUARY : BALCONY SW DOORS

The name of God is the *Yod*, Hebrew initial for Jehovah. Superimposed on a *chi rho*, sacred monogram for Jesus Christ. The burning bush that revealed God to Moses is a symbol of God's presence.

SANCTUARY : BALCONY SW DOORS

The cup of suffering of the agony of Gethsemane
that Jesus accepted as His Father's will.

SANCTUARY : BALCONY SW DOORS

Six loaves and two fish that made up a boy's lunch
was multiplied by Jesus to feed the five thousand.

SANCTUARY : BALCONY SW DOORS

The scales of justice are unequally balanced, but God's hand extends in forgiveness.

SANCTUARY : BALCONY NW DOORS

The *fasces* of the *lictor*, a bag of money and the laurel wreath, symbolize the temptations of the world from which the staff of the Good Shepherd protects mankind.

SANCTUARY : BALCONY NW DOORS

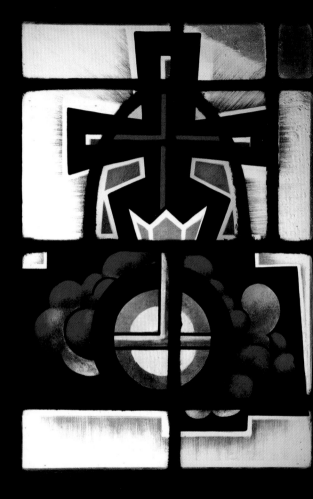

A cross rises triumphantly above the serpent of evil.

SANCTUARY : BALCONY NW DOORS

The cross-topped orb is the symbol of the triumph of Christianity over the world. Together with a crown it denotes royalty.

Rejoice in the Lord always; again I will say, Rejoice.

PHILLIPPIANS 4:4

PEWS FEATURE THE RELIEF CARVING OF THE
SYMBOL OF THE NUMBER THREE REPRESENTING
THE TRINITY.

FAITH

The author of Hebrews defines faith as the assurance of things hoped for but unseen. Our faith is often tested through loss of a loved one, illness, disappointment in our professional lives, betrayal of our trust, or prayers that seem to go unanswered. Like Thomas, we want to see and touch. We want quick responses and answers from God. Then, we will have faith.

If you find yourself in Thomas' shoes, may your faith be strengthened and renewed by these stories of faith found at First Presbyterian.

HANGING CROSS

The hanging cross above the chancel is a Celtic cross and represents the sacrifice made by Christ. The architects were A. Hensel Fink, Philadelphia. The cross was crafted by Allied Crafts Company, Philadelphia. The cross weighs 450 pounds and is fifteen feet long.

Mrs. Walter (Mary Ellen) Esser and daughters Mrs. Sue Amstutz and Mrs. Sherye Jeanne Halliburton gave the cross in memory of Mr. Walter (Bill) Esser.

JOHN 19:17–18

Jesus said to the woman, "Your faith has saved you; go in peace."

LUKE 7:50

BUST OF JESUS HEALING
THE BLIND MAN

*Gift of Dr. George and
Virginia Krietmeyer*

MARK 8:22–25
MATTHEW 9:29

49

PROCESSIONAL CROSS:
The Alpha and Omega imposed on a circle, the Cross of Triumph.

Designed by Geordie Matson and the Ziegler Company and crafted by the Ziegler Company. The wrought iron repeated the material and design of the portion of the old pulpit and lectern.

Gift of Geordie and Laurie Matson to honor their parents Daphne and George Matson in 2002.

JOHN 19:17–18

NEEDLEPOINT CUSHIONS:
Winged man Matthew 4:24
Winged lion Mark 11:22
Winged ox Luke 7:50
Winged eagle John 5:27

The ivy around the edge is evergreen and represents eternal life. The Roman numerals are 1885, the year First Church was founded.

The needlepoint cushions were crafted by a committee of members including Anne McCune, Amy Dodson, Diane Miller, Frances Patterson, Willie Hodges, Marcia Lansdown, Susan Diacon, Jean Lemmon, Jackie Allen, Pam Shaeffer and Ruth Huffman.

THE FOUR EVANGELISTS

The medallion window above features a cross pate with "Y" crosses representing the Holy Trinity. The four transoms on the following page include symbols of Matthew, Mark, Luke and John and an inscription from the Gospel of each illustrating faith. The symbols are derived from the four beasts that are described in the fourth chapter of Revelation.

ABOVE : Matthew is given the winged man for he describes Jesus' human nature.

According to your faith be it unto you. Matthew 9:29

Sanctuary : entrance transom

BELOW : Luke tells of Jesus' sacrificial nature so his is the animal of sacrifice, the ox.

Thy faith hath saved thee. Luke 7:50

Sanctuary : entrance transom

ABOVE : Mark's beast is the winged lion for his Gospel opens with the voice of one crying in the wilderness.

Have faith in God. Mark 11:22

Sanctuary : entrance transom

BELOW : John's is the most inspirational Gospel which seems to ascend to heaven like the eagle on strong wings.

He that believeth hath everlasting life. John 5:24

Sanctuary : entrance transom

ACTS OF CHRISTIAN MERCY

The Alpha and the Omega — the beginning and the end
— enclose the symbols of mercy that Christians are to
extend to those in need: food, water, hospitality, clothing,
medication and visitation.

Donated by Annelle Chandler McAdams
Installed in late 1979

Matthew 25:35–40

Transom in the vestibule of
Kerr Memorial Building

Abel's more acceptable sacrifice, a lamb.

The three crosses of Calvary recall another person who had faith that Christ could save him. This was the penitent thief who shared His death.

Luke 23:39–43

Abraham's attempted sacrifice of his son Isaac shown by the funeral pyre, the knife, and a ram caught in the bush by its horns.

GENESIS 22:9–14

SANCTUARY : MAIN FLOOR SW DOORS

The waters of the Red Sea part to allow Moses to lead the children of Israel through and away from captivity.

EXODUS 14:21–25

SANCTUARY : MAIN FLOOR NW DOORS

The trumpets of Joshua blow and the walls of Jericho fall down.

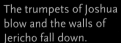

JOSHUA 6:20

The child Moses set adrift amid the
rushes in a basket boat by his mother.
The pyramids of Egypt are behind.

Healing of the centurion's servant is
symbolized by the master's helmet and
the servant's bed.

The man by the pool at Bethesda is typified by his pallet beside the waves.

JOHN 5:2–9

SANCTUARY : MAIN FLOOR N DOORS

Noah's ark

GENESIS 6:14–16

A witness that He was truly the Son of God was the centurion who watched him die on the cross. Above is the inscription I.N.R.I. – Jesus of Nazareth, King of the Jews.

MATTHEW 27:54

SANCTUARY : MAIN FLOOR N DOORS

The Savior's hand reaches out to

Peter was said to have been crucified

HEALING OF THE BLIND
MAN

MARK 10:46–52;
MATTHEW 20:29–34

OPPOSITE : CHRIST
BLESSING THE
CHILDREN

MATTHEW 18

*Donated by Annelle
Chandler McAdams.*

Installed September,
1979.

KERR CHAPEL

FOLLOWING PAGE:

PROCESSIONAL CROSS
Designed and crafted by
Bill Derrevere. Symbols
include the lamb, dove
and light.

KERR MEMORIAL BUILDING

THE CALVARY CROSS
The Calvary Cross is set on
three graded steps, which
stand for faith, hope, and
love.

MILLER LIBRARY

CROSS
Crafted by Tim Clement

Gift of Bob and Sandy Curti
and Bill and Glenna Hailey
in honor of their fathers:
Thomas Newton Deane,
Walter Jackson Curtis, Dick
Tull and Woodrow W. Hailey

BERNSEN COMMUNITY LIF
CENTER

THE BEATITUDES

West and southwest door transoms
Virtues and Fruits of the Spirit

Willet Stained Glass Studios, Inc. Installed 1984–85 I Corinthians 13:13

The iconography of these two transom windows contain symbols that may be less well known in the Christian Church. They are based on the Greek concept of dividing human behavior philosophically into virtues and vices that eventually found its way into Christianity via the Beatitudes. An early church scholar, Ambrose, used the word "cardinal" in describing the virtues on which the lesser virtues are based. Thomas Aquinas refined the list.

left : Fruits of the Spirit
Love – heart
Joy – bells
Peace – olive branch
Patience (long suffering) – spider web
Goodness – keys to the kingdom
Meekness – yoke
Wisdom – owl
Knowledge – lamp
Healing – serpent on staff
Working miracles – five loaves
    and two fish
Prophecy and interpretation
    of tongues – a scroll

Galatians 5:22–23 and
I Corinthians 12:7–10

above : The Cardinal Virtues
Temperance – a compass
Justice – scales
Fortitude – a broken column
Prudence – a padlock

The Theological Virtues
Faith – a cross
Hope – an anchor
Charity – a cup of water

The Morality Virtues
Courage – breastplate
Vigilance – rooster
Liberality – cornucopia
Purity – lily

SACRAMENTS & CELEBRATIONS

Sacraments are outward signs – symbols – of inner grace.

The Presbyterian church celebrates two sacraments, those of baptism and communion. Through baptism, we are made pure, our sins cleansed, and we are born anew. Baptism is the symbolic act of resurrection.

Communion, the Lord's Supper, the Eucharist, reminds us of the sacrifice Jesus Christ made for us dying on the cross. When we take the bread and drink from the cup, we follow Christ's instructions to "do this in remembrance of me."

There is a time for everything, and a season for every activity under heaven . . .

ECCLESIASTES 3:1

ASCENSION
MARK 16:19–20
ACTS 1:9
LUKE 24:50–53

Installed September, 1979

Donated by Annelle Chandler McAdams

The SACRAMENT OF BAPTISM combines a number of symbolic acts. Water, or the act of washing, cleans and purifies and is a symbol of innocence. In baptism, the water washes away the sins of the past, with rebirth and regeneration to follow. The initials on the font are the first letters of the Greek words for Jesus. The quatrefoil carved on the font represents the four gospels.

Gift of the Percy Collins Class

COLOSSIANS 2:12

COMMUNION TABLE holds the elements of the Last Supper, "this you do in remembrance of me." In the Reformed tradition, the church does not have an altar as the sacrifice has already been made.

KERR CHAPEL BAPTISMAL FONT
COLOSSIANS 2:12

THE SACRAMENT OF COMMUNION

COMMUNION SERVICE

Paten – round tray that holds the communion bread

Chalice (cup) – the container that holds the communion wine

above : Bernsen Community Life Center communion service
created by Bill Derrevere

Wedding cushion

COLUMBARIUM

The First Church columbarium is an arrangement of some 700 recessed niches dedicated to the glory of God and in grateful memory of those who have died in Christ. The columbarium serves as an extension of the ancient Christian custom of burying the dead within the "Kirkyard."

The gate with Celtic cross motif offers both an invitation to enter and protection from the outside world.

The fountain reminds us of the baptism, cleansing of Jesus, the Living Water. The sphere speaks of eternity and the wholeness in eternity that the one Lord God gives.

Jesus said, "I am the resurrection and the life. Those who believe in me, even though they die, yet will they live." John 11:25.

FPC Columbarium Committee: Bill Stewart, chair; Allan and Vivienne Edwards, Marge Glenn, Janie Long, George and Daphne Matson, Jim Sneed, and Audrey Tucker.

Architect: Olsen-Coffey Architects.
Construction Manager: Will Keith, Keith Construction.
Dedicated Sunday, September 12, 2004

Reredos (chancel screen)

The panel separates the chancel area from the choir loft and is adorned with a decorative motif of intertwined vines, representing the True Vine and the grape, a symbol of the Eucharist. A descending dove represents the Holy Spirit. The slender pinnacles decorated with the crocket (hooks) remind us of the staff of the Good Shepherd.

TAU CROSS: The Greek letter *Tau* is often called the "Cross of Prophecy" and is associated with God's promise given through His prophets of a coming Messiah.

FIVE-POINTED STAR: The Epiphany Star is a symbol of the nativity. The star tells of Christ Jesus' coming, his birth.

CHALICE: The chalice is a symbol of communion and commemorates the Last Supper.

CROWN OF THORNS WITH THREE (3) NAILS: The crown is symbolic of Christ's suffering and crucifixion.

PHOENIX: The phoenix is a mythical bird that was said to burst into flames at death but rise again, reborn, from its own ashes. It is a symbol for the resurrection.

DRIPPING SHELL: The dripping shell is symbolic of the baptism of Jesus.

CHI AND RHO: The Greek letters *Chi* and *Rho* are the first letters in the Greek word for Christ. The letters over the mountain represent the transfiguration of Christ.

FLEUR-DE-LIS: The fleur-de-lis is a symbol for purity and is often used to represent Mary, mother of Jesus. The three petals of the fleur-de-lis represent the trinity.

LATIN CROSS RESTING ON A GLOBE: The Latin cross resting on a globe is called the cross triumphant and is symbolic of Christ's ascension and his lordship over the world.

MONEY BAG: Thirty pieces of silver arch above the money bag to symbolize Judas and the betrayal of Christ.

PURPLE, THE COLOR OF PENITENCE AND EXPECTATION, IS USED IN THE SEASONS OF ADVENT AND LENT.

WHITE SYMBOLIZES JOY, PURITY AND TRUTH, AND IS USED ON WEDDING DAYS AND FOR FUNERALS. IT SYMBOLIZES HOLINESS. THE COLOR IS USED ON THE HOLIEST OF DAYS.

THE STOLE/VESTMENTS

The stole, worn by the clergy, follows the colors of the paraments, and symbolizes the yoke of Christ, of humility. It also represents the towel used in foot washing.

RED, THE COLOR OF FIRE AND BLOOD, IS USED ON PENTECOST, ORDINATION AND GOOD FRIDAY.

GREEN, THE COLOR OF LIVING THINGS, IS USED DURING "ORDINARY TIME." IT REPRESENTS THE GROWTH OF THE CHRISTIAN CHURCH.

THE LIFE OF CHRIST

COUNTERCLOCKWISE:

The First Christmas
LUKE 2:1–20

Jesus and the Teachers in the Temple
LUKE 2:46–49

Jesus Welcomes the Children
MATTHEW 19:13–15

Sermon on the Mount
MATTHEW 5, 6, & 7

Jesus Learns to be a Good Workman
(shown in window, lower center)
MARK 6:3 ; MATTHEW 13:55

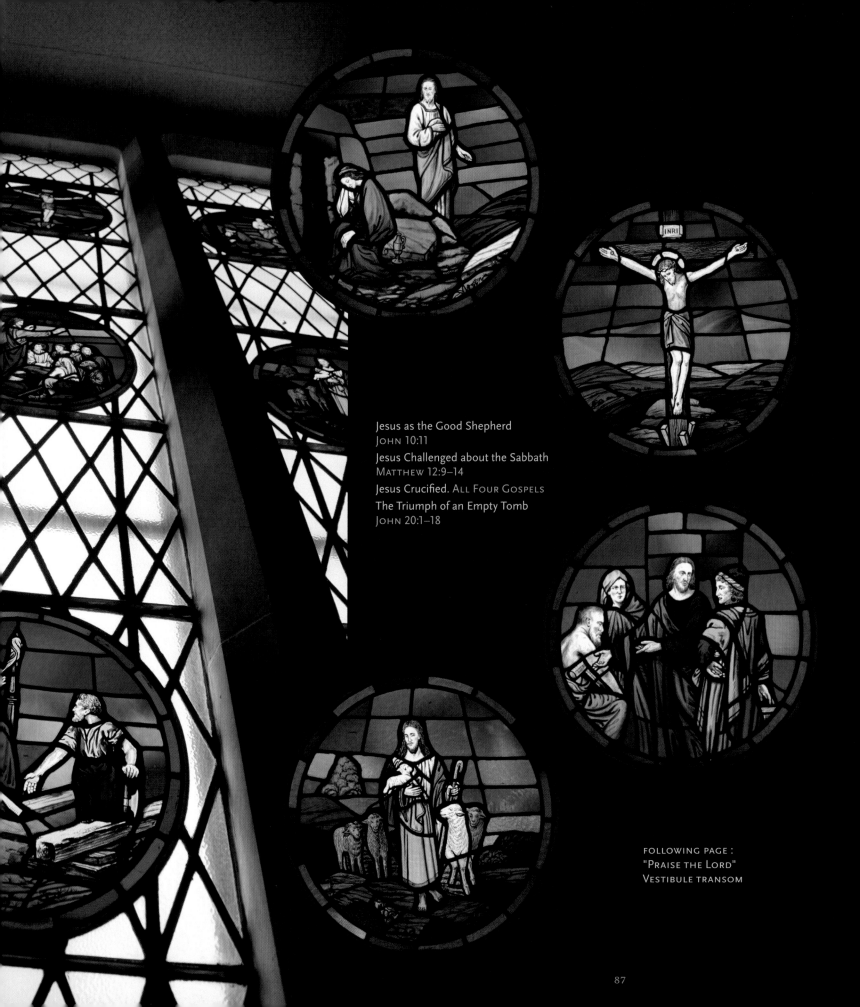

Jesus as the Good Shepherd
JOHN 10:11
Jesus Challenged about the Sabbath
MATTHEW 12:9–14
Jesus Crucified. ALL FOUR GOSPELS
The Triumph of an Empty Tomb
JOHN 20:1–18

FOLLOWING PAGE :
"PRAISE THE LORD"
VESTIBULE TRANSOM

EPILOGUE
LIGHTING OUR FUTURE

First Presbyterian Church of Tulsa, the city's first church, has changed remarkably since 1885. Driven by the power of our vision statement—*Called to make fully-devoted followers of Jesus—Inwardly Strong and Outwardly Focused*—First Presbyterian has maximized its current campus. To further enable His work, as we serve current and future generations, ground was broken on May 30, 2010 for facility expansion. Renovation and preservation of our 1925 English Gothic sanctuary and Kerr Memorial Building and the addition of new spaces will continue our shining legacy in the community.

With the Lord as our guide, our congregation embarks on the next stage of our commitment to serve and witness to our Lord Jesus Christ locally and globally. First Church believes God is at work every day, changing minds and hearts and transforming human lives for the glory of God. Our mission is to live in such a way that all we do and say today and in the future shall be for the glory of God.

ABOVE : LOCATED ON THE EXISTING ALLEY AND PORTICO, THE STUNNING NEW COMMONS AREA IS A PLACE OF GATHERING. IT CONNECTS EVERY BUILDING AND PROVIDES STAIR AND ELEVATOR ACCESS TO EVERY LEVEL OF THE CHURCH. IT IS DESIGNED TO BRING IN AS MUCH LIGHT AS POSSIBLE WITHOUT BLOCKING ANY LIGHT TO THE SANCTUARY'S CHRIST, THE "LIGHT OF THE WORLD" WINDOW.

AERIEL VIEW FROM EIGHTH AND CINCINNATI OF THE NEW WORSHIP CENTER ON THE LEFT AND THE NEW CLASSROOM AND OFFICE WING ON THE RIGHT.

TOP RIGHT : THE NEW ENTRY PORTICO CONNECTING THE EXISTING SANCTUARY WITH THE NEW WORSHIP CENTER. BOTTOM RIGHT : NEW EAST ENTRY ON CINCINNATI AVENUE OPENING TO THE COURTYARD AND CONNECTING SPACES FOR THE NEW WORSHIP CENTER, CLASSROOMS AND OFFICES, AND THE EXISTING SANCTUARY AND KERR MEMORIAL BUILDING.

BELOW : AERIAL VIEW OF THE PRESENT SANCTUARY AND KERR MEMORIAL BUILDING FROM SEVENTH AND BOSTON.

GLOSSARY

The words and terms listed below are by no means a complete catalog of religious terms, but those that may be helpful in understanding the liturgical art at First Presbyterian Church.

ANGELS — God's messengers

ANCHORS — symbol for cross, salvation, hope, constancy

APOSTLES — twelve men who became Christ's primary missionaries sent forth to preach the Gospel

ASHES — penance, the transitory nature of life

BELT/GIRDLE — humility, chastity

BREAD — the body of Christ

CANDLE — Christ, the "Light of the World"

CHANCEL — raised area in front of sanctuary for preaching, teaching, and music

CHI RHO — the first two letters of the Greek word for Christ

CHURCH — the people of God, the Body of Christ, the fellowship of the Holy Spirit; place of worship, the house of God; a place of salvation, it may be represented by a ship

CORD — with three knots, the Trinity; worn by monks to recall the flagellation of Jesus

CROCKET — ornate protrusion (hook) on slender upward extension, often shape of shepherd's crook

CROSS — the universal symbol for Christ and Christianity

EASTER — Resurrection of Jesus

EUCHARIST — Holy Communion, the Last Supper, bread and wine, Lord's Supper; Christ's body and blood

EVANGELISTS — bearers of good news; Gosple writers Matthew, Mark, Luke and John

FIRE — religious fervor, martyrdom, Pentecost, Holy Spirit

FLAG — with red cross, victory; with lamb, Christ's victory over death; resurrection banner

FOUNTAIN — salvation; Jesus, the well of living water

GOD THE FATHER — represented by large hand emerging from clouds; bearded man

GOD THE SON — represented by lamb, fish, cross, good shepherd

GOD THE HOLY SPIRIT — represented by dove, tongue of flames

HALO — holy people, supernatural light

HARP — King David, Jesus' ancestor; all music that glorifies God

INRI — Latin letters, Jesus of Nazareth, King of the Jews

KEYS — attribute of St. Peter, keys to the kingdom

LITURGY — an order of worship

LITURGICAL YEAR — the seasons observed by the Christian church

Advent — begins four Sundays before Christmas; a time of preparation

Christmas — Birth of Christ

Transfiguration of the Lord — Sunday before Ash Wednesday

Ash Wednesday — seventh Wednesday before Easter; ashes from the previous year's palms are used as a token of penance

Lent — forty days, excluding Sundays; represents days spent by Moses, Elijah and Christ in the desert; a waiting time, preparation for Easter

Holy Week — Palm Sunday, Maundy Thursday, Good Friday, Holy Saturday and Easter Sunday; represent the entry of Jesus into Jerusalem, trial, death and resurrection

Easter

Ascension — forty days after Easter

Pentecost

Trinity Sunday — Sunday after Pentecost

Christ the King — Last Sunday before the end of liturgical year

Ordinary time — all other times of year

MOON — the passage of time, fullness of time; the Virgin Mary

NARTHEX — gathering area at entry to sanctuary

NAVE — the central area of sanctuary flanked by pews

OIL — consecration, anointment

PATEN — shallow circular plate that holds the bread

PARAMENTS — liturgical hangings from the pulpit and lectern

PENTECOST — forty days after Easter when the Holy Spirit descended

RAINBOW — reassurance, pardon, forgiveness, reconciliation; God's covenant with Noah

REREDOS — ornamental panel or screen behind the pulpit

ROPE — Judas, who hanged himself after betraying Christ

SANCTUARY — place of worship, sanctity, sacred space

SHELL/SCALLOP — with drops of water baptism, the Lord's baptism

SHIP — the Church; the ark that saved believers from destruction

SPQR — Latin *Senatus Populusque Romanus* (the Senate and the people of Rome)

SUN — Christ

VESTMENTS — garments worn by clergy; robe and stole

Stole — humility, service, towel; the yoke of Christ

WATER — purity, innocence, salvation; baptism; Christ

LAMP MEDALLION

SYMBOLS IN LITURGICAL ART

Colors, numbers, shapes, articles, animals and plants have traditionally been used in liturgical art to represent or indicate persons, emotions, or specific characteristics. Listed below are those most basic to understanding the artists' meanings.

COLORS

WHITE – purity, innocence, virginity, faith, light; the color for weddings, funerals, and communion; nativity, transfiguration, resurrection; Eastertide

BLACK – mourning, penance, death

RED – passion, blood, fire; Good Friday, Pentecost, ordination; Holy Spirit

BLUE – heaven; spiritual love, truth, fidelity; the color for Mary

GREEN – regeneration, hope, new life, fertility, growth, victory

PURPLE OR VIOLET – sorrow and penitence, but also love and truth; worn by Mary after the crucifixion; royalty; Advent and Lent

BROWN OR GRAY – humility, mortification, mourning; often worn by monks

YELLOW OR GOLD – God; divinity, light; illuminated truth and divine intelligence

NUMBERS

ONE – divinity and unity

TWO – dual nature of Christ, both human and divine

THREE – Trinity

FOUR – Gospels

FIVE – wounds of Christ

SIX – days of creation

SEVEN – Sabbath, the day of rest; man (spirit and body)

EIGHT – regeneration, new life, resurrection, wholeness

NINE – nine choirs of angels

TEN – perfection (Trinity and man)

SHAPES

CIRCLE – God's perfection; three entwined represent the Trinity

OCTAGON – eight represents regeneration

PENTAGRAM – five wounds of Christ

QUATREFOIL – four Gospels

SQUARE – earth, square halo represents a living person, earthly aspects, i.e. compass, stability

TREFOIL – Trinity

TRIANGLE – Trinity

PLANTS

The shape and color of the plant often serves as meaning applied to both color and number.

HOLLY – the Passion; the crown of thorns

LAUREL – victory, immortality

CLOVER (3 LEAF) – Trinity

IRIS (FLEUR-DE-LIS) – symbol for purity, often used to represent Mary, mother of Jesus; three petals represent the Trinity

LILY OF THE VALLEY – Immaculate Conception, purity, the flower of Mary

ROSE – white (purity), red (martyrdom), yellow (impossible perfection); Mary

Five-petal rose: five joys of Mary; five letters of her name, Maria

VIOLET – humility

APPLE – Adam and Eve; sin, the fall

FIG – lust; fertility; knowledge

GRAPES – wine; abundance; the Eucharist

IVY – eternal life

LEMON – fidelity in love, often with Mary

ORANGE – chastity

NUTS – fertility

POMEGRANATE – eternity; fertility

STRAWBERRY – fruits of the spirit; righteousness; trefoil leaf represents the Trinity

VINE – Jesus, the true vine

TREES

CEDAR – Christ

CYPRESS – death

OAK – strength, longevity; firmness of faith in God

OLIVE – God's generosity

PALM – triumph and victory

ANIMALS

ASS OR DONKEY – humble, long-suffering, docile

BEE – creativity, wealth, industry

BUTTERFLY – new life, resurrection

COCK – vigilance, alertness

DOG – fidelity

DOVE – Holy Spirit; the soul leaving the body; purity and peace

EAGLE – resurrection and Christian spirit; represents John

FISH – sign of faith, Christ, baptism; the net, a symbol of the church

GOLDFINCH – crown of thorns; the passion, as the bird eats thistle

LAMB – sacrificial animal, Jesus; with Christ the Good Shepherd

LION – strength, valor, courage; winged lion represents Mark

MAN – represents Matthew

OWL – wisdom; death, night, solitude

OX – sacrificial animal, represents Luke

PEACOCK – immortality

PHOENIX – resurrection

SNAKE/SERPENT – evil, Satan, wisdom; God's authority

SPIDER – fragility of human nature; evil

SWALLOW – spring, resurrection

SANCTUARY

STAINED GLASS

Chancel Window

CHRIST, THE "LIGHT OF THE WORLD"

Christ stands at the door of our hearts knocking to enter and the only door handle is on the inside.

This window replaced the original window of the same design based on the famous painting by William Holman-Hunt, *The Light of the World.*

Mr. D. J. Tuepker gave the Chancel Window in memory of his wife, Ardyth Tuepker.

Installed the week of December 4, 1967 following renovation of 1965–67.

Dedication held on January 12, 1969.

Pgs 14–17

Door Lights

PARABLES

Symbols of parables are nearest the pulpit, which is the source of teaching.

Pgs 27–31

PRAYER AND PRAISE

The symbols of upper west balcony are of prayer and praise. In the four side doors are musical instruments: trumpets, a harp, a violin and triangle and cymbals. The eight openings in the main rear balcony contain symbols of the Lord's Prayer.

Pgs 40–43

STORIES OF FAITH

In the sixteen openings in the lower rear doors are the stories of faith, some of which are recounted in the eleventh chapter of Hebrews.

Pgs 56–61

Installed December 10, 1969.

Transoms

MATTHEW, MARK, LUKE AND JOHN

The four transoms include symbols of Matthew, Mark, Luke and John and an inscription from the Gospel of each illustrating faith. The symbols are derived from the four beasts which are described in the fourth chapter of Revelation.

Pgs 52–57

Sanctuary West Window

WISEMAN ROSE

Donated by Bill Wiseman Jr. in honor of Dr. William Wiseman.

Installed 1996

Pg vi

THE GOOD SHEPHERD

Frederick J. Wiley, Paris & Wiley, New York. After a painting by Bernhard Plockhorst 1825–1907

Mr. E.P. (Earl) Harwell was a deacon and on the building committee of our current sanctuary. Frank Barnes was chairman and J.M. Chandler, vice-chairman.

It is part of the original 1925 building.

Pgs 32, 33

MEDALLIONS

A shield with a large cross and initials IHS in the center is surrounded by four smaller crosses in the corners, forming the St. Andrew's Cross. A wreath, composed of leaves, flowers and crown, encloses the shield. Opposite page.

A shield contains the symbols IHC/IHS with the crown. The letters are the first three letters of Greek for Jesus. The Crown is symbolic of the Lord's kingship. The eight pointed star symbolizes regeneration. The Star of David represents Jesus' lineage.

The roses, crowns, and circles in all medallions have the same meaning (pgs 96, 97). The leaves and grape refer to Christ, the True Vine, and wine of communion. The lily is the flower of Mary and represents purity and innocence.

The shield with the chalice represents the agony in Gethsemane. A small cross, known as the Cross of Suffering, appears out of the chalice.

The chalice and cross represent the same as in the previous image.

The large cross serves to subdivide the names of the four Evangelists. Pg 51

The Lamb of God, representing Christ himself, carries a white banner with red cross symbolize victory. Pg 32

The harp symbolizes the glorification of God and is a symbol of praise. Pg 7

The dove represents the Holy Spirit. It may also be the symbol of peace.

The shield includes the cross pate, the tree or Westminster cross and the symbol for the four evangelists.

The quill pens in the center of the shield represent the four evangelists and his gospel.

The lamp represents wisdom (wise and foolish virgins), piety, intelligence. Pg 92

West Entry Transoms

VIRTUES

FRUITS OF THE SPIRIT

Installed 1984–85.

Willet Stained Glass Studios, Inc.

Pgs 68–69

SHIELD MEDALLION

SANCTUARY : WEST END UPPER GALLERY

Elevator Lobby

THE GOOD SAMARITAN

THE SOWER SEEDS

Ann Willet Stained Glass Atelier, Spring House, Pennsylvania

The windows given to the Glory of God in memory of beloved family members by Annelle Chandler McAdams, 1985
Installed 1984.

Pgs viii, x

Prayer Room

To the Glory of God, this window is dedicated to the loving memory of George and Armenta Davis

CROSSES

HANGING CROSS

The architect of this Celtic cross was A. Hensel Fink, Philadelphia; crafted by Allied Crafts Company, Philadelphia.

Gift of Mrs. Walter (Mary Ellen) Esser and daughters, Mrs. Sue Amstutz and Mrs. Sherye Jeanne Halliburton in memory of Mr. Walter (Bill) Esser.

Pg 18, 46

PROCESSIONAL CROSS

Designed by Geordie Matson and the Ziegler Company; crafted by the Ziegler Company.

Gift of Geordie and Laurie Matson in honor of Daphne and George Matson in 2002.

Pg 50

CELTIC CROSS

Pg 19, 20

SCULPTURE

EAGLE

Symbol of the resurrection of the Christian spirit. Created by artists William R. Derrevere, Paul Moore and Dewayne Pass.

Pgs 20–21

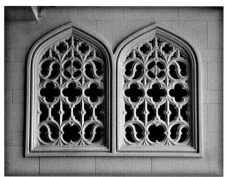

FIXTURES/ARCHITECTURAL DETAILS OF THE PRESENT BUILDING

THE SANCTUARY

First Presbyterian Church was organized on October 5, 1885. Mrs. Kerr (Annie), wife of our first pastor, determined the design of the current building, English Gothic, and monitored the construction. The architect was J.A. Parr, Oklahoma City. J.M. Berry was chairman of the trustees at the dedication in 1925.

The sanctuary features many of the Gothic elements including: the nave, representing the ship of salvation; the transept forming the arms of a cross; high ceiling with pointed arch; and light streaming through windows on all four walls. Modified Roman arches define the balcony and columns provide visual support at the east end. The Corinthian motif of the acanthus leaf carries out the classical theme on the support columns along the north and south sides.

Pgs 2–3, 4–5, 6–7, 12–13, 18–19, 44–45, 48, 66–67

PULPIT

The pulpit is in the center of the chancel raised above all seating as this is where the word of God is spoken. The three arches relief are a repetitive motif inside each arch around the pulpit base. The eight sided octagon shape represents the resurrection.

The original pulpit was a gift of Mr. and Mrs. Lawrence L. Dresser.

Pgs 2–3, 20, 84–85

REREDOS (CHANCEL SCREEN)

Pgs 82–83

BAPTISMAL FONT

Gift of the Percy Collins Class.

Pgs 72, 4–5

COMMUNION TABLE

Pgs 72–73, 74

COMMUNION SERVICE

Paten – round tray that holds the communion bread
Chalice – the cup that holds the communion wine

Pgs 2, 74

EAGLE LECTERN

Gift of Jim Dixon. Given to the glory of God and in loving memory of Sarah and Wilton O. Dixon by their son, James P. Dixon.

Installed October 28, 2001.

Pgs 20–21

PEWS

Pews feature the relief carving of the symbol of the number three representing the Trinity.

Pgs 2–3, 44–45

CHANDELIERS (bronze)

The chandeliers repeat the Gothic design and have the quatrefoil used in the cut-outs.

Gift of Mr. and Mrs. Donald Parm Moyers, in memory of their son, Captain Robert Parm Moyers

Pgs 2–3, 64

DOOR HARDWARE

Hardware on doors, in both the sanctuary and chapel, repeats the Gothic design.

MUSICAL INSTRUMENTS

THE SANCTUARY ORGAN

The organ was built by Austin Organs, Inc. Hartford, Connecticut

Gift of Mr. and Mrs. Robert C. Sharp. Dedicated January 12, 1969, with guest performer Frederick Swann, organist of the Riverside Church, New York City.

Pgs 5, 10–11

THE CONTINUO ORGAN

Located at the rear of the sanctuary.

Given in 1993 in memory of his parents by William H. Shambaugh.

Pg 8

PIANO

The Sanctuary piano is a Steinway, Model B; 1989.

CARILLON BELLS

A thirty-two, bronze-bell carillon cast by the Fonderie Paccard of Annecy, France.

Major donors to the acquisition were Doris Maher and Patricia Wheeler.

Pg 11

HANDBELLS

The bells were made by the Whitechapel foundry in England.

The set of handbells on display in the Miller Library were given in 1962 by Mrs. Robert H. Wood and sons Harold and Robert, in memory Mr. Robert H. Wood.

TEXTILES

PARAMENTS

The color of this textile is determined by the church calendar.

THE STOLE/VESTMENTS

The stole, worn by the clergy, follows the colors of the paraments, and symbolizes the yoke of Christ, of humility.

Pgs 84–85

NEEDLEPOINT CUSHIONS

The ivy around the edge is evergreen and represents eternal life. The grapes and staffs of wheat represent the body and blood of Christ. The Roman numerals are 1885, the year First Church was founded.

The needlepoint cushions were crafted by a committee of members including Anne McCune, Amy Dodson, Diane Miller, Frances Patterson, Willie Hodges, Marcia Lansdown, Susan Diacon, Jean Lemmon, Jackie Allen, Pam Shaeffer and Ruth Huffman.

The Gospels

MATTHEW, MARK, LUKE, JOHN Pg 50

CUP OR CHALICE

The Lord's Supper.

THE TRINITY

Three intertwined fish.

SHIP

The church, the ship of salvation.

SHELL

The Lord's baptism.

WEDDING CUSHION

Pgs 84–85

NARTHEX

STAINED GLASS

Transom and Rose Window

Installed 1981.

Gift of Mr. and Mrs. David (Cassie) Temple.

Pgs i, xii, xvi, 88–89

Four Single Lancet Windows

JESUS IS TAKEN TO THE TEMPLE
   BY HIS PARENTS

JESUS TEACHES A LESSON OF FAITH
   CONSIDER THE LILIES

JESUS WORSHIPS IN THE TEMPLE
   ON THE SABBATH

JESUS IN THE TEMPLE WITH TEACHERS

Installed 1981.

Pgs 34–35

Double Lancet Gothic Window

JESUS AND NICODEMUS

JESUS IN THE HOME OF MARY
   AND MARTHA

Installed 1981.

Pg 37

East Wall Alcove

THE ALPHA AND OMEGA

Designed by the Ann Willet Stained Glass Atelier of Springhouse, Pennsylvania. Installed 1983.

Pg 36

SCULPTURE

BUST OF JESUS HEALING THE BLIND MAN

Given by Dr. George and Virginia Krietmeyer

Pg 49

THE NICENE CREED

THE APOSTLES' CREED

THE SCOTS CONFESSION

KERR MEMORIAL BUILDING

STAINED GLASS

West Entrance Transom

ACTS OF CHRISTIAN MERCY (OUR BONDED DUTY)

The Alpha and the Omega — the beginning and the end — enclose the symbols of mercy that Christians are to extend to those in need: food, water, hospitality, clothing, medication and visitation.

Donated by Annelle Chandler McAdams.
Installed in late 1979.

Pgs 54–55

Chapel Medallion Windows

NATIVITY

CHRIST BLESSING THE CHILDREN

HEALING OF THE BLIND MAN

ASCENSION

Donated by Annelle Chandler McAdams
Installed September 1979.

East Entrance Hallway

THE GOOD SHEPHERD

Dedicated to the memory of the Presbyterian Women who, since 1885, have been witnesses to the promise of God's kingdom.

Donated by Presbyterian Women

THE GOOD SHEPHERD

West Stairwell

THE LIFE OF CHRIST
(lowest to highest levels)

THE FIRST CHRISTMAS

JESUS LEARNS TO BE A GOOD WORKMAN

JESUS AND THE TEACHERS IN THE TEMPLE

JESUS WELCOMES THE CHILDREN

SERMON ON THE MOUNT

JESUS AS THE GOOD SHEPHERD

JESUS CHALLENGED ABOUT THE SABBATH

JESUS CRUCIFIED

THE TRIUMPH OF AN EMPTY TOMB

Pgs 86–87

CROSSES

Hallway

PROCESSIONAL CROSS

Designed and crafted by Bill Derrevere. Symbols include the lamb, dove and light.

Pg 64

Chapel

THE LATIN CROSS

Created, crafted and donated by Dr. George Coe.

Pg 38

Library

THE CALVARY CROSS

Pg 64

MUSICAL INSTRUMENTS

Chapel

ORGAN

Gift of Mr. and Mrs. David (Sara Ann) Burton, in memory of her parents, Mr. and Mrs. Edward Sloan.

Dedicated in 1975.

The first organ in the Kerr Chapel was given by the Mr. and Mrs. Class in May 1954.

Pg 9

THE HEIDELBERG CATECHISM

THE WESTMINSTER CONFESSION AND THE SHORTER CATECHISM

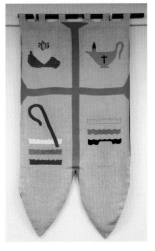

THE SECOND HELVETIC CONFESSION

Piano

The Kerr Chapel piano is a Steinway Model 1098.

Gift of Mr. and Mrs. Class, 1989.

TEXTILES

Chapel

THE GOOD SHEPHERD TAPESTRY

The Good Shepherd tending flock of sheep in field. It was added to collection during the chapel renovation in the 1990s.

Wiesman Hall

The confessional banners were made by Pam Shaeffer. A companion set was presented to Matanzas Seminary, Cuba, during the second mission trip, 2002.

THE NICENE CREED (Fourth Century)

Cross – the doctrine of Christ, which is central to the creed

Reaching hand – God

Descending dove – the Holy Spirit

Crowns – the rule and glory of God

Chi Rho – letters for Christ

THE APOSTLES' CREED

Purple arches – the entrance to caves

Anchor cross – security in Christ

Fish – the ancient symbol of Christians and their faith

Chalice – the container for the wine served at the Last Supper

Inverted cross – the apostle Peter, who was crucified upside-down

THE SCOTS CONFESSION (Scotland 1560)

Blue shield with tartan, X-shaped cross and St. Andrew's Cross (Celtic cross) – the Church of Scotland

Hamilton plaid – the first martyr of the Scottish Reformation, Patrick Hamilton

Ship – the church

Bible and sword – Paul's definition of the word of God, "the sword of the Spirit"

Burning bush – the chief symbol of the Church of Scotland, recalls Moses and the burning bush which reminds us of God's presence

THE HEIDELBERG CATECHISM (Germany, 1563)

Red and gold – tribute to the rule of Frederick III, who ordered the writing of the catechism for followers of John Calvin in Germany

Crown of thorns, the cross and the tablets – misery, redemption and thankfulness; themes of the catechism

Lights and fire with writing – the Hebrew name of God, and the Greek monogram for Jesus

THE SECOND HELVETIC CONFESSION (Switzerland, 1566)

Blue and white – heraldic colors of ancient Switzerland

Cross – salvation

Hand and burning heart – John Calvin, father of Presbyterianism

Lamp – knowledge and discipline

Shepherd's crook and the pasture – pastoral ministry and the flock's care for its own members

Chalice and waves – Holy Communion and Baptism

THE WESTMINSTER CONFESSION AND THE SHORTER CATECHISM (England, 1646)

Three panels – the Trinity

Eye – God's providence and control of all life and history

Crown – God's rule

Alpha and Omega – first and last

THE THEOLOGICAL DECLARATION OF BARMAN (Germany, 1934)

Swastika crossed out and cross rising – a protest and witness against Nazi tyranny and its effort to take the role of God and control the church

Fire – suffering and death which follows from defense of the faith against tyranny, but the cross survives

THE CONFESSION OF 1967 (USA)

Blue, red and gold – official colors of the Presbyterian Church (USA)

Crown – God's rule

Nail-scarred hand – death and victory of Christ

Four hands of different colors, the clasped hands and the green circle – reconciled world at the foot of the cross

Stars and planets – space-age setting of this confessional

THE THEOLOGICAL
DECLARATION OF BARMAN

THE CONFESSION OF 1967

West Entry Staircase

PRESBYTERIAN WOMEN BANNERS:
THE TRIAD (PEACE, JOY AND LOVE)

Joy ascends, flows upward to embrace all.
The seven-fold flame reaches upward and
is the symbol of the Holy Spirit reaching to
encompass all humankind.

Love embodies the Christian doctrine of
the Transcendence of God. The symbol in
the center, the three circles, represents the
Holy Trinity. The color green represents
birth, growth, hope, development and
maturation.

Peace includes the Descending Dove, a
symbol of the Holy Spirit and of our Peace
from God. The color blue represents the
sky, vastness and infinity.

*The banners, created by Pam Shaeffer, are
in honor of three Presbyterian Women who
faithfully served in PW: Nadine Wilson,
Winifred S. Chick and Ruth Lupton.*

FIXTURES/ARCHITECTURAL DETAILS

PULPIT

The pulpit in the chapel is located on the
south with the lectern on the north, an
unusual arrangement in the Presbyterian
Church.

Pgs 22–23

CHANDELIERS (bronze)

Similar to the Sanctuary, repeat the Gothic
design with quatrefoils.

BERNSEN COMMUNITY LIFE CENTER

CROSS

Crafted by Tim Clement

*Gift of Bob and Sandy Curtis and Bill and
Glenna Hailey in honor of their fathers:
Thomas Newton Deane, Walter Jackson
Curtis, Dick Tull and Woodrow W. Hailey.*

Pg 65

SCULPTURE

DIVINE SERVANT

Jesus washing the feet of Peter
Created by Max Greiner Jr.
Bronze, cast by Eagle, Lander, Wyoming.

Gift of the Garvin Berry family

FIXTURES/ARCHITECTURAL DETAILS

PULPIT, MADE FOR THE 75TH ANNIVERSARY

Replica of an early pulpit made by Rev.
Ralph Lamb and carried across the
Arkansas River from Red Fork.

Pg 22

COMMUNION SET

Created by Bill Derrevere

Pg 75

BAPTISMAL STAND/FONT

Crafted by Ray Hedgecock out of a walnut
log recovered from a sandbank of the Little
River in southwest Arkansas.

COLLECTION PLATES

Designed by Tim Clement.
Hand-turned walnut and brass.

MUSICAL INSTRUMENTS

Great Hall

Pianos

Steinway Model B
Gift of Dick and Barbara Horkey, 1998.

Knabe, Model WKG 70
Gift of the Southmayd family, in memory of
Sybil Southmayd, 2008.

Lewis Room:

Piano

Boston, Model GP 178
Gift of Ray and Jean Hedgecock, 1998.

EXTERIOR

Columbarium

Columbarium Committee: Bill Stewart,
chairman; Allan and Vivienne Edwards,
Marge Glenn, Janie Long, George and
Daphne Matson, Jim Sneed and Audrey
Tucker.
Architect: Olsen-Coffey Architects.
Construction Manager: Will Keith, Keith
Construction.

Dedicated Sunday, September 12, 2004.

Pgs 78–79

West Façade

The architectural features of the Gothic-
style building includes three main doors,
representing the Trinity, relief sculpture of
crosses, unadorned shields or breastplates,
and adorned shields of a light/lamp and
cross with banner.

Christmas Eve
J. Johnson
Gift by the artist in 2006.

SCRIPTURAL REFERENCES

NOTE : *Italic text* indicates scripture specific to the artwork.

ACTS

1:9 | When he had said this, as they were watching, *he was lifted up, and a cloud took him out of their sight.* (pg 71)

COLOSSIANS

2:12 | *. . . when you were buried with him in baptism, you were also raised with him through faith in the power of God, who raised him from the dead.* (pgs 4–5 , 72, 73)

I CORINTHIANS

11:25–26 | *This cup is the new covenant in my blood. Do this, as often as you drink it, in remembrance of me." For as often as you eat this bread and drink the cup, you proclaim the Lord's death until he comes.* (pgs 2, 74, 75, 82, 101)

12:7–10 | *To each is given the manifestation of the Spirit for the common good. To one is given through the Spirit the utterance of wisdom, and to another the utterance of knowledge according to the same Spirit, to another faith by the same Spirit, to another gifts of healing by the one Spirit,* to another the working of *miracles*, to another *prophecy*, to another the *discernment of spirits*, to another various kinds of *tongues*, to another the *interpretation of tongues*. (pg 69)

13:3 | *So faith, hope, love/charity abide, these three; but the greatest of these is love.* (pg 68)

II CORINTHIANS

4:5 | *For we do not proclaim ourselves: we proclaim Jesus Christ as Lord and ourselves as your slaves for Jesus' sake.* (pgs 19, 20, 22–23)

EPHESIANS

4:4–6 | *There is one body and one Spirit, just as you were called to the one hope of your calling, one Lord, one faith, one baptism, one God and Father of all, who is above all and through all and in all.* (pg 83, 101)

EXODUS

14:21–25 | Then Moses stretched out his hand over the sea. The LORD drove the sea back by a strong east wind all night, and turned the sea into dry land; and the waters were divided. The Israelites went into the sea on dry ground, the waters forming a wall for them on their right and on their left. *The Egyptians pursued, and went into the sea after them, all of Pharaoh's horses, chariots, and chariot drivers. At the morning watch the LORD in the pillar of fire and cloud looked down upon the Egyptian army, and threw the Egyptian army into panic. He clogged their chariot wheels so that they turned with difficulty.* (pg 57)

2:1–3 | Now a man from the house of Levi went and married a Levite woman. The woman conceived and bore a son; and when she saw that he was a fine baby, she hid him three months. *When she could hide him no longer she got a papyrus basket for him, and plastered it with bitumen and pitch; she put the child in it and placed it among the reeds* on the bank of the river. (pg 58)

GALATIANS

5:22–23 | *By contrast, the fruit of the Spirit is love, joy, peace, patience, kindness, generosity, faithfulness, gentleness, and self-control . . .* (pg 68)

GENESIS

4:4 | *. . . and Abel for his part brought of the firstlings of his flock, their fat portions. And the LORD had regard for Abel and his offering,* (pg 56)

6:14 | *Make yourself an ark of cypress wood; make rooms in the ark, and cover it inside and out with pitch.* (pg 59)

22:9–13 | When they came to the place that God had shown him, *Abraham built an altar there* and laid the wood in order. He bound his son Isaac, and laid him on the altar, on top of the wood. Then Abraham reached out his hand and took the knife to kill his son. But the angel of the LORD called to him from heaven, and said, "Abraham, Abraham!" And he said, "Here I am." He said, "Do not lay your hand on the boy or do anything to him; for now I know that you fear God, since you have not withheld your son, your only son, from me." *And Abraham looked up and saw a ram.* (pg 57)

HEBREWS

13:4 | *Let marriage be held in honor by all, . . .* (pgs 76–77)

ISAIAH

43:2 | *When you pass through the waters, I will be with you; and through the rivers, they shall not overwhelm you . . .* (pgs 24, 101)

JOHN

3:1 | *Now there was a Pharisee named Nicodemus, a leader of the Jews.* (pg 37)

4:13–14 | Jesus said to her, *"Every one who drinks of this water will be thirsty again, but those who drink of the water that I will l give them will never be thirsty; the water that I give them will become in them a spring of water gushing up to eternal life."* (pg 17)

4:25 | Jesus said to them, *"Very truly, I tell you, before Abraham was, I am."* (pg 17)

5:2–9 | *Now in Jerusalem by the Sheep Gate there is a pool, called in Hebrew Beth-zatha,* which has five porticoes. *In these lay many invalids*-blind, lame, and paralyzed. *One man was there who had been ill for thirty-eight years.* When Jesus saw him lying there and knew that he had been there a long time, he said to him, "Do you want to be made well?" The sick man answered him, "Sir, I have no one to put me into the pool when the water is stirred up; and while I am making my way, someone else steps down ahead of me." Jesus said to him, "Stand up, take your mat and walk." At once the man was made well, and he took up his mat and began to walk. (pg 59)

5:24 | *Very truly, I tell you, anyone who hears my word and believes him who sent me has eternal life, and does not come under judgment, but has passed from death to life.* (pg 53)

6:35 | Jesus said to them, *"I am the bread of life. Whoever comes to me will never be hungry, and whoever believes in me will never be thirsty.* (pgs 2, 17, 72–73, 74,75)

6:51 | *I am the living bread that came down from heaven. Whoever eats of this bread will live for ever; and the bread that I shall give for the life of the world is my flesh."* (pg 17)

8:12 | Again, Jesus spoke to them, saying, *"I am the light of the world. Whoever follows me will never walk in darkness but will have the light of life."* (pg 17)

10:7 | So Jesus again said to them, *"Truly, truly, I say to you, I am the door of the sheep."* (pg 17)

10:11 | *"I am the good shepherd. The good shepherd lays down his life for the sheep."* (pgs 33, 67, 87, 102)

10:36 | . . . because I said, *"I am God's Son"* (pg 17)

11:1 | *Now a certain man was ill, Lazarus of Bethany, the village of Mary and her sister Martha.* (pg 37)

11:25–26 | Jesus said to her, *"I am the resurrection and the life. Those who believe in me, even though they die, will live, and whoever lives and believes in me shall never die. Do you believe this?"* (pgs 17, 78)

13:4–5 | . . . [Jesus] *got up from the table, took off his outer robe, and tied a towel around himself. Then he poured water into a basin and began to wash the disciples' feet and to wipe them with the towel that was tied around him.* (pg 104)

13:14–16 | "So if I, your Lord and Teacher, have washed your feet, you also ought to wash one another's feet. For I have set you an example, that you also should do as I have done to you. *Very truly, I tell you, servants are not greater than their master, nor are messengers greater than the one who sent them."* (pg 104)

14:6 | Jesus said to him, *"I am the way, and the truth, and the life. No one comes to the Father, except by me."* (pg 17)

15:1 | *"I am the true vine, and my Father is the vine grower."* (pgs 2, 17, 74–75)

17:24–25 | *"Father, I desire that they also, whom you have given me, may be with me where I am, to see my glory which you have given me because you loved me before the foundation of the world. you, Righteous Father, the world does not known you* but I know you; and there know that you sent me." (pg 17)

19:17–18 | So they took Jesus; *and carrying the cross by himself,* he went out to what is called The Place of the Skull, which in Hebrew is called Golgotha. There they crucified him, and with him two others, one on either side, with Jesus between them. (pgs 19, 38, 46, 50, 64–65, 82, 83)

20:1 | Early on the first day of the week, while it was still dark, *Mary Magdalene came to the tomb and saw that the stone had been removed from the tomb.* (pg 87)

20:17 | Jesus said to her, "Do not hold on to me, because I have not yet ascended to the Father. But go to my brothers and say to them, 'I am ascending to my Father and your Father, to my God and your God.'" (pg 70)

JOSHUA

6:20 | So the people shouted, and the trumpets were blown. *As soon as the people heard the sound of the trumpets, they raised a great shout, and the wall fell down flat;* so the people charged straight ahead into the city and captured it. (pg 56–57)

LUKE

2:6–7 | While they were there, the time came for her to deliver her child. *And she gave birth to her firstborn son and wrapped him in bands of cloth, and laid him in a manger, because there was no place for them in the inn.* (pg xiv , 86)

2:41 | *Now every year his parents went to Jerusalem for the festival of the Passover.* (pg 35)

2:46 | *After three days they found him in the temple, sitting among the teachers, listening to them and asking them questions.* (pgs 35, 86)

2:49 | *He said to them, "Why were you searching for me? Did you not know that I must be in my Father's house?"* (pg 35)

4:16–22 | When he came to Nazareth, where he had been brought up, he went to the synagogue on the Sabbath day, as was his custom. He stood up to read, and the scroll of the prophet Isaiah was given to him He unrolled the scroll . . . (pg 34)

5:18–20 | *Just then some men came, carrying a paralyzed man on a bed.* They were trying to bring him in and lay him before Jesus; but finding no way to bring him in because of the crowd, *they went up on the roof and let him down with his bed through the tiles* into the middle of the crowd in front of Jesus. When he saw their faith, he said, "Friend, your sins are forgiven you." (pg 58)

7:50 | *And he said to the woman, "Your faith has saved you; go in peace."* (pgs 50, 51, 52)

10:29–34 | But wanting to justify himself, he asked Jesus, "And who is my neighbor?" Jesus replied, "A man was going down from Jerusalem to Jericho, and fell into the hands of robbers, who stripped him, beat him, and went away, leaving him half dead. Now by chance a priest was going down that road; and when he saw him, he passed by on the other side. So likewise a Levite, when he came to the place and saw him, passed by on the other side. *But a Samaritan while traveling came near him; and when he saw him, he was moved with pity.* He went to him and bandaged his wounds, having poured oil and wine on them. (pg viii)

10:38 | Now as they went on their way, he entered a certain village, where a woman named Martha welcomed him into her home. (pg 37)

11:2–4 | Father, hallowed be your name. Your kingdom come. Give us each day our daily bread. And forgive us our sins, for we ourselves forgive everyone indebted to us. And do not bring us to the time of trial." (pgs 40–43)

15:4 | "Which one of you, having a hundred sheep and loosing one of them, does not leave the ninety-nine in the wilderness and go after the one that is lost until he finds it"? (pg 30)

22:42 | *"Father, if you are willing, remove this cup from me; yet, not my will but yours be done."* (pg 99)

23:39–40 | *One of the criminals who were hanged there kept deriding him* and saying, "Are you not the Messiah? Save yourself and us!" *But the other rebuked him,* saying, "Do you not fear God, since you are under the same sentence of condemnation?" (pg 56)

24:50-53 | Then he led them out as far as Bethany, and, lifting up his hands, he blessed them, while he was blessing them, he withdrew from them and was carried up to heaven . . . (pg 71)

MARK

6:3 | *Is this not the carpenter's son, the son of Mary and brother James and Joseph and Judas and Simon, and are not his sisters here with us?* (pgs 86–87)

8:22–25 | *They came to Bethsaida. Some people brought a blind man to him and begged him to touch him.* He took the blind man by the hand and led him out of the village; and when he had put saliva on his eyes and laid his hands on him, he asked him, "Can you see anything?" And the man looked up and said, "I can see people, but they look like trees, walking." *Then Jesus laid his hands on his eyes again; and he looked intently and his sight was restored, and he saw everything clearly.* (pg 49, 60)

10:44 | *. . . and whoever wishes to be the first among you must be slave of all.* (pg 104)

10:46 | They came to Jericho. As he and his disciples and a large crowd were leaving Jericho, *Bartimaeus son of Timaeus, a blind beggar, was sitting by the roadside.* (pgs 49, 62)

11:22 | *Jesus answered them, "Have faith in God"* . . . (pgs 24, 50, 51, 53)

MATTHEW

4:24 | *So his fame spread throughout all Syria, and they brought to him all the sick, those who were afflicted with various diseases and pains, demoniacs, epileptics, and paralytics, and he cured them . . .* (pg 50)

5:1–12 | *When Jesus saw the crowds, he went up the mountain; and after he sat down, his disciples came to him. Then he began to speak, and taught them, saying:*

"Blessed are the poor in spirit, for theirs is the kingdom of heaven.
Blessed are those who mourn, for they will be comforted.
Blessed are the meek, for they will inherit the earth.
Blessed are those who hunger and thirst for righteousness, for they will be filled.
Blessed are the merciful, for they will receive mercy.
Blessed are the pure in heart, for they will see God.
Blessed are the peacemakers, for they will be called children of God.
Blessed are those who are persecuted for righteousness' sake, for theirs is the kingdom of heaven.
Blessed are you when people revile you and persecute you and utter all kinds of evil against you falsely on my account. Rejoice and be glad, for your reward is great in heaven, for in the same way they persecuted the prophets who were before you." (pg 87)

6:9–13 | *Pray then in this way:*
"Our Father in heaven,
hallowed be your name.
Your kingdom come.
Your will be done,
on earth as it is in heaven.
Give us this day our daily bread.
And forgive us our debts,
as we also have forgiven our debtors.
And do not bring us to the time of trial, but rescue us from the evil one.
(pgs 40–43)

6:26–29 | Look at the birds of the air; they neither sow nor reap nor gather into barns, and yet your heavenly Father feeds them. Are you not of more value than they? And can any of you by worrying add a single hour to your span of life? And why do you worry about clothing? *Consider the lilies of the field, how they grow; they neither toil nor spin, yet I tell you, even Solomon in all his glory was not clothed like one of these.* (pg 34)

7:24–27 | "Everyone then who hears these words of mine and acts on them will be like a wise man who built his house on rock. *The rain fell, the floods came, and the winds blew and beat on that house, but it did not fall, because it had been founded on rock.* And everyone who hears these words of mine and does not act on them will be like a foolish man who built his house on sand. *The rain fell, and the floods came, and the winds blew and beat against that house, and it fell—and great was its fall!"* (pg 27)

8:1–5 | What do you think? *If a shepherd has a hundred sheep, and one of them has gone astray, does he not leave the ninety-nine on the mountains and go in search of the one that went astray?* (pg 30)

8:5–7 | When he entered Capernaum, *a centurion came to him, appealing to him and saying, "Lord, my servant is lying at home paralyzed, in terrible distress."* And he said to him, "I will come and cure him." (pg 58)

9:9 | As Jesus was walking along, *he saw a man called Matthew sitting at the tax booth; and he said to him, "Follow me."* And he got up and followed him. (pg 61)

9:17 | "Neither is new wine put into old wineskins; otherwise, the skins burst, and the wine is spilled, and the skins are destroyed; *but new wine is put into fresh wineskins,* and so both are preserved." (pg 29)

9:18 | While he was saying these things to them, *suddenly a leader of the synagogue came* in and knelt before him, saying,
"My daughter has just died; but come and lay your hand on her, and she will live."(pg 49, 62)

9:20–22 | Then suddenly *a woman who had been suffering from hemorrhages for twelve years came up behind him and touched the fringe of his cloak,* for she said to herself, "If I only touch his cloak, I will be made well." Jesus turned, and seeing her he said, "Take heart, daughter; your faith has made you well." And instantly the woman was made well. (pg 60)

9:29 | *Then he touched their eyes and said, "According to your faith let it be done to you."* (pgs 49)

12:9–10 | He left that place and entered their synagogue; a man was there with a withered hand, and they asked him, *"Is it lawful to cure on the sabbath?"* so that they might accuse him. (pg 87)

13:3–9 | And he told them many things in parables, saying: "Listen! *A sower went out to sow.* And as he sowed, some seeds fell on the path, and the birds came and ate them up. Other seeds fell on rocky ground, where they did not have much soil, and they sprang up quickly, since they had no depth of soil. But when the sun rose, they were scorched; and since they had no root, they withered away. Other seeds fell among thorns, and the thorns grew up and choked them. Other seeds fell on good soil and brought forth grain, some a hundredfold, some sixty, some thirty. Let anyone with ears listen!" (pg x)

13:31–32 | He put before them another parable: "The kingdom of heaven is like a mustard seed that someone took and sowed in his field; it is the smallest of all the seeds, but when it has grown it is the greatest of shrubs and *becomes a tree, so that the birds of the air come and make nests in its branches."* (pg 31)

13:33 | He told them another parable: *"The kingdom of heaven is like yeast that a woman took and mixed in with three measures of flour until all of it was leavened."* (pg 29)

13:47–48 | "Again, *the kingdom of heaven is like a net that was thrown into the sea and caught fish of every kind;* when it was full, they drew it ashore, sat down, and put the good into baskets but threw out the bad. (pg 31)

13:55 | *Is this not the carpenter's son?* (pg 86–87)

19:14 | . . . but Jesus said, *"Let the little children come to me,* and do not stop them; for it is to such as these that the kingdom of heaven belongs." (pg 63, 86)

25:1–13 | "Then the kingdom of heaven will be like this. Ten bridesmaids took their lamps and went to meet the bridegroom. *Five of them were foolish, and five were wise. When the foolish took their lamps, they took no oil with them; but the wise took flasks of oil with their lamps."* (pg 28)

25:14–18 | "For it is as if a man, going on a journey, summoned his slaves and entrusted his property to them; to one he gave five talents, to another two, to another one, to each according to his ability. Then he went away. *The one who had received the five talents went off at once and traded with them, and made five more talents. In the same way, the one who had the two talents made two talents. But the one who had received the one talent went off and dug a hole in the ground and hid his master's money."* (pg 28)

25:31–32 | "When the Son of Man comes in his glory, and all the angels with him, then he will sit on the throne of his glory. *All the nations will be gathered before him, and he will separate people one from another as a shepherd separates the sheep from the goats . . ."* (pg 30)

25:35–40 | "'. . . *for I was hungry and you gave me food, I was thirsty and you gave me something to drink, I was a stranger and you welcomed me, I was naked and you gave me clothing, I was sick and you took care of me, I was in prison and you visited me.'* Then the righteous will answer him, 'Lord, when was it that we saw you hungry and gave you food, or thirsty and gave you something to drink? And when was it that we saw you a stranger and welcomed you, or naked and gave you clothing? And when was it that we saw you sick or in prison and visited you?' And the king will answer them, 'Truly I tell you, just as you did it to one of the least of these who are

members of my family, you did it to me.'" (pgs 54–55)

27:54 | *Now when the centurion and those with him, who were keeping watch over Jesus, saw the earthquake and what took place, they were terrified and said, "Truly this man was God's Son!"* (pg 59)

MATTHEW 28:1-7 | But the angel said to the womn, "Do not be afraid; I know that you are looking for Jesus who was crucified. He is not here; for he has been raised, . . . (pgs 86–87)

28:19 | *Go therefore and make disciples of all nations, baptizing them in the name of the Father and of the Son and of the Holy Spirit . . .* (pg 101)

II PETER

1:14 | . . . *since I know that my death will come soon, as indeed our Lord Jesus Christ has made clear to me.* (pg 61)

PSALMS

148:1 | *Praise the LORD!*
Praise the LORD from the heavens;
praise him in the heights! (pgs i, xii, xvi, 88–89)

148:12 | . . . *Young men and women alike, old and young together!* (pg xii)

148:14 | *He has raised up a horn for his people* (pg xvi)

150:3–6 | *Praise him with trumpet sound; praise him with lute and harp!* Praise him with tambourine and dance; praise him with strings and pipe! Praise him with clanging cymbals; praise him with loud clashing cymbals! Let everything that

breathes praise the LORD!
Praise the LORD! (pgs 7, 8, 9)

REVELATION

4:7 | . . . *the fourth living creature like a flying eagle . . .* (pg 20–21)

22:13 | *"I am the Alpha and the Omega, the first and the last, the beginning and the end."* (pg 17)

ROMANS

8:38–39 | *For I am convinced that neither death, nor life, nor angels, nor rulers, nor things present, nor things to come, nor powers, nor height, nor depth, nor anything else in all creation, will be able to separate us from the love of God in Christ Jesus our Lord.* (pgs 78–79)

PHOTOGRAPHY CREDITS

FIRST PRESBYTERIAN CHURCH
TULSA † OKLAHOMA